A Quilt for Charley

Based on a True Story

Sharon Winters

Illustrated by Toby Mikle

For information about this title or to order other books and/or electronic media, contact the publisher:

Sharon Winters
www.SharonWinters.com

ISBNs:
979-8-9861004-9-4 (hardcover)
979-8-9895372-0-4 (softcover)
979-8-9895372-1-1 (eBook)

Printed in the United States of America

Illustrations by Toby Mickle: www.MyBookIllustrator.com

Dedicated to all of the people who are committed to rescuing animals and finding them forever loving homes. In particular:

The Humane Society of Yuma
in Yuma, Arizona

Friends for Life Animal Rescue
in Gilbert, Arizona

Maricopa County Animal Care and Control
in Mesa and Phoenix, Arizona

My name is Charley. A man found me wandering in a park and brought me to a dog shelter.

Maricopa County
Animal Care and Control

At the shelter, someone took my picture.

Next, I met a doctor who listened to my heart and checked my eyes and ears. He saw a big scar on my forehead and wondered what had happened to me that gave me such a big scar. Then someone put me into a cage.

4

I have been here for many weeks in a kennel with a bed and a door that goes outside. There are about fifty dogs that are also in kennels. A lot of people go up and down the aisle of the kennels, but no one stops to look at me.

Some dogs are taken out of their kennel, and they go to forever homes. Or sometimes the owner of a dog comes and takes their dog home. When owners find their dog at the shelter, they are so happy. My former family hasn't come to take me home. Why don't they want me?

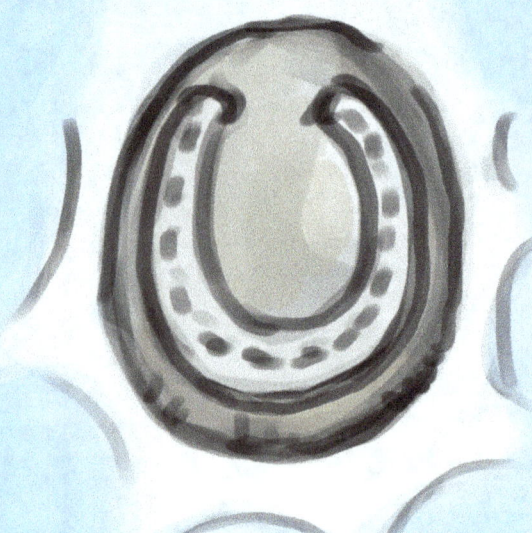

Even though there are a lot of dogs here, I feel alone. The other dogs are all excited and bark when someone comes down the aisle. I don't bark about anything. I feel sad. No one wants me.

I'm about nine years old. That's old for a dog. I'm a big dog, too. I weigh eighty pounds, and I have a big scar on my forehead. No one here seems to know what happened to me, but I remember. I was kicked by a horse! My life hasn't been an easy one.

There is a nice woman who feeds all of us breakfast and dinner. When she puts down my bowl of kibble, she says, "Don't give up hope, Charley. You will find a loving home. You are a gentle giant and a handsome boy." She is the only person who thinks I'm handsome.

One night I had a dream. A chocolate-colored dog with golden eyes walked into my dream. This dog said, "Hey Charley, of all the dogs in all the towns in all the world, I have chosen you to go to a special forever home. Your hard life is over. The love in this home will fill your heart with happiness.

"Tomorrow, your new mommy and daddy will come to take you home. Look into their eyes with all of the love you have in your heart, and all will be right with the world."

8

When I woke up this morning, I remembered my dream and the chocolate-colored dog with the golden eyes, and this afternoon my caretaker stopped by the door to my kennel. She attached a leash to my collar and said, "Here's your chance, Charley, to have a good home. Two people want to meet you."

9

My caretaker took me out to a grassy yard where there was a man and a woman. When the woman saw me, she said, "I love his face!"

10

I walked up to her and looked into her eyes just like the chocolate-colored dog told me to do. She said, "I want this dog," as she touched my face and ears.

I went up to the man, and he touched me with gentleness and said, "Okay, let's take him home."

My new mommy and daddy filled out adoption papers at the county clerk's desk. My caretaker took me out to a big car. I felt scared.

My new mommy was in the back seat, and all the way home she talked to me and petted me. I put my paws on her legs and rested my face between my paws until we were home.

My dinner was a beef burger, gravy, and doggy kibble.

It was soon time for bed.
Mommy showed me my bed,
which was a large, round, soft bed.

On Mommy's and Daddy's bed was a large quilt.
I went over to the quilt and tried to pull it off.

Mommy said, "Charley, this quilt is not for you."

Even though my bed was soft and comfortable, I wanted a quilt, too.

Mommy gave me some blueberry-yogurt treats before bed, and I went to sleep.
But not for long.

18

I cried and howled. Daddy got up and gently woke me up. He asked, "What's the matter, Charley? You are having a bad dream. Let's go outside for a while."

HOWLLLLLLL

The air was warm, and when I looked at the sky, there were a lot of stars.

20

When Daddy took me back into the bedroom, I again glanced at the quilt. I really wanted a quilt for my bed, too. I know . . . that quilt is not for me.

21

In the morning, Daddy took me outside to my new backyard. When I came back into the house, I glanced at another quilt that was on the back of a couch. I know . . . that quilt is not for me.

Mommy brought me into the bathroom where she brushed my fur and took a washcloth with warm water and rubbed it over my eyes and ears and then my neck and back. That felt so good. After she put a special cream on my scar, she said, "Charley, you are ready for the day, and all is right with the world."

Yes, all is right with the world, except . . . that quilt is not for me.

I love my new backyard . . . but then I saw a large hot air balloon with some people in it. I didn't want the noisy balloon to land in my new yard, so I barked at it until it went away. Mommy said, "Charley, you saved the whole neighborhood from that hot air balloon!"

I had a wonderful day and soon, it was time for bed. I walked into the bedroom and glanced at the quilt . . . not for me. I liked having my face washed, so I walked into the bathroom, took the washcloth from the cabinet door, and dropped it in front of Mommy's sink.

Mommy picked up the washcloth and put it back.

Daddy said, "Charley wants you to wash his face again."

Mommy washed my face with warm water on a washcloth, and I went to bed after getting treats. I glanced at the quilt, but it was not for me.

This morning, all the neighborhood dogs were barking, and Daddy asked, "Charley, what do you have to say to all of those barking dogs?" I went outside and barked one big, deep, and loud WOOF! All of the dogs went silent. Daddy laughed and said, "Good boy, Charley. You told them you are the boss of the neighborhood!"

Many weeks went by, and I was happy . . . until there was a knock on the door. A man said, "Okay, Charley. It's time for you to go to school."

No, Daddy! No, Mommy! Don't let him take me away!

Mommy came over to me and kissed my forehead.
"Everything will be alright, Charley. You will be back with us
in no time at all! I love you, Charley." Daddy came over to me.
"You will be okay, Charley. We will see you again soon." Daddy
rubbed my face and ears, and the man took me away.   27

School was a lot of work for me, but the man who was my teacher was kind to me. After several weeks, my teacher said, "Charley, you have worked hard and earned a special vest. Let's put your vest on and take you home." The vest said: SERVICE DOG.

When my teacher rang the doorbell, Daddy answered the door and yelled out to my mommy, "Charley is here!" Daddy said, "Charley, we are so proud of you! Now you are Mommy's service dog."

Mommy put her hands on my face and kissed my forehead as she said, "We missed you, Charley. You are such a good boy. And now you can always be with me."

It was good to be back home. At bedtime, Mommy washed my face, I ate my treats, and I went to my bed. Mommy left the room, and Daddy looked toward the door. Mommy came in with a quilt, and I sat up in my bed. Mommy and Daddy each held a corner of the quilt so I could see it. Daddy said, "Mommy made this quilt, and this quilt is for you, Charley!"

I went over to the quilt. Wowzah! This quilt is for me!

Daddy put the quilt on my bed. I stepped onto my bed with the quilt. This quilt was soft. This quilt was made just for me. All is right with the world.

Charley and His Quilt

photography by Hatton Pet Portrait Studio

About the Author

photo by Hatton Pet Portrait Studio

SHARON WINTERS holds a BS in psychology from Illinois State University and an MA in humanities from the University of Texas. A retired English and math teacher, Winters is the author of:

Cutted Chicken in Shanghai—an award-winning humorous memoir that explores the time the author spent living in China.

Runtie the Desert Rat—a picture book that tells a touching story about the wonders of nature and a desert rat with a problem to solve.

Karl's Diary: It's a Dog's Life—written from a dog's perspective, this memoir won the Literary Titan Gold Book Award granted to well-written books with great stories.

A Quilt for Charley—a heartfelt true story about a rescued dog who wants a quilt of his own. This picture book resonates with children and adults alike, and is a winner of the Literary Titan Gold Book Award, the Readers' Favorite Five Star Award, and the Reader Views Silver Medal Reviewers Choice Award.

Winters' stories have appeared in *The Rodent Reader Quarterly* and in several national and international Mensa publications. She is currently working on her fifth book, *Stories from Here and There*. Winters lives with her service dog, Charley, and her husband in the Phoenix area. When she is not writing, she enjoys quilting and playing the piano. Find her online at www.SharonWinters.com

32

About the Artist

TOBY MIKLE has been passionately illustrating books for the past twenty years with more than nine hundred titles. He illustrated his first book at age fourteen for his English teacher who had written a story about a bear. His work was so well received that he soon began creating books for other teachers and friends. After a stint in the Air Force and earning a degree from a local art school, Toby began working professionally in his chosen field.

Toby's books have been published in seven different countries and in many languages. His custom award-winning illustrations underscore his colorful ability to entertain the active imagination of children. You can find a portfolio of his work at www.MyBookIllustrator.com